THE P

SERIES

Series Titles

Praise for

Glitter City

"The poems in Bonnie Jill Emanuel's *Glitter City* are photographic. Their tension pulls between urban darkness and the green lights of floral and plant life. The thread of losses is a bridge between these. People in the shadows, vines reaching vines, the communion among strangers in the city, vulnerability, illness, and the haunting early days of the Covid pandemic are almost like voices in the poems. The poems' shapes and leaps show the tenderness of nature, but also its blind viciousness. Emanuel's eye for texture and surprising insights in poem after poem mean she is always listening."

—Sean Singer
author of *Today In The Taxi*

"'At the center/of it all is the heart,' writes Bonnie Jill Emanuel in her sorrowful and astounding collection of poems, *Glitter City*. These poems allow and are allowed. Sit down and read them in the dark and you will be able to see. The light is in every one of her missives because she writes from the center. It is the heart of these poems, whether you are walking with the speaker through Brooklyn or the shores of Lake Erie, that let you love. Love. Can you say love anymore when talking about poems? I love these poems and I don't care if you can or not. Because when you read these poems, you feel them in your body. Yes. You feel these beauties everywhere in the physical matter of your being. Bonnie Jill Emanuel's poems glitter. They glitter Taraxacum, they glitter 8-Mile Road, they glitter '*I am Neil Armstrong in an avalanche*,' they glitter all the cities and factories and love stories of a whole world. *Glitter City*—in all its shapes and forms and heartbeats—glitters you, glitters me, glitters the blood river of the human spirit that never wants to stop shining."

—Matthew Lippman
author of *We Are Sleeping with Our Sneakers On*

"The best way to see a star is to gaze at the sky beside it, so its shape and shimmer sidle into your eye. In the spare, intense, searching, sometimes sidelong poems of *Glitter City*, Bonnie Jill Emanuel writes in burst after burst of light, her images and insights accruing into seriously dazzling designs of illumination. Even as her urban and natural landscapes are lit by shadows, by what is 'alive & perishing/at once,' they glint with human connection and the hard-won comprehension of beauty. 'Love is sky./Rejoice like a weed every hour,' she says. In another poem she declares, 'the sky itself grows as I write.' For the reader, these poems emerge one by one like evening stars that ultimately trace entire constellations."

—David Groff
author of *Live in Suspense*

"The glitter in Bonnie Jill Emanuel's poetry is a starry break from the expected. She enlists these tiny shards to pierce what's ordinary and illuminate it—making a novel experience of something as common as sorrow or a field of fences or a convenience store's torn awning. The world, in her imagination, takes place in a kind of metaphoric 3-D. There's a wildness and depth to her range, her palette. Her *heart*, like glitter, is so far from sentimental she gets it to glide into fresh emotional territory with subtly and ease, as in: 'The heart always feels so humid/in the eyes' and '… I drop my heart down the soapy dark dishwater lake to see if it still floats.' In poem after nimble poem, *Glitter City* is that rarity—a true and sustained pleasure to read."

—Elaine Sexton
author of *Drive*

GLITTER CITY.

BONNIE JILL EMANUEL

CORNERSTONE PRESS
UNIVERSITY OF WISCONSIN-STEVENS POINT

Cornerstone Press, Stevens Point, Wisconsin 54481
Copyright © 2024 Bonnie Jill Emanuel
www.uwsp.edu/cornerstone

Printed in the United States of America by
Point Print and Design Studio, Stevens Point, Wisconsin

Library of Congress Control Number: 2023951980
ISBN: 978-1-960329-32-5

Cornerstone Press titles are produced in courses and internships offered by the
Department of English at the University of Wisconsin–Stevens Point.

For Henry, Peter, & Julian.

CONTENTS

ONE

TWO

GLITTER CITY.

ONE

O

The shimmer of the wind
gliding across the land with the dandelion
seeds, flax-yellow florets
under dead or blinking traffic lights
running   running   down Avenue A.

Shepherd's Purse, amaranth.

Rats *clack* the fire escape.

Zoom me
the sun on your tongue.

I'll whisper a blue glitter field
to my screen—
                    it will zoom
right back to you.

O Desolate.

O Bloom.

In the Squall I Think Washington Square Park Is a Jackson Pollock

After "Mural" (1943)

                *

A whiteout
        all shiny perfect

& a fatal plague.

Then would come another.
                *
            I circle the square
            with what's left
            of my heart

                    winter blue cold
            falling through me.

            People look
        like the squall itself
                    dark slants this way
            & that

doing what they can
            in their knife bodies
& long coats

        a frenzy of bags
        loaves of bread
        bottles of velvety things

                    splotch of yellow here
            blood-orange there.

One guy stopped
          cold flicks a lighter

cigarette arrowing
     from his thin
          frown mouth.

                              Trace of crows
                         blur into milky white
                              arch   & vanish.

          *

     I once loved
     a painting so much

     I think
     I'm trying to tell you

               about dancers
               in a casein grave

               alive & perishing
               at once.

Dear Winter,

All day the sky the same
colorless grey as rock
salt, truck-scattered over
Fulton Street.

Trees leafless darker
shades of bark.

I walk.   Cross
DeKalb to the hospital
where people wait
& wait.

Lines to get shots.

A blankness
fills the air bundled
like a quilt of longing
& time.

Fluffy dog on a leash
in the crosswalk
turns to me with her wet nose
        as if pondering
too or expecting
something.

   Always might
begin flurrying again.

Dirty yellow taxis
circle glass
emergency room door.

I slip my mask down
just a few seconds—

      take a cold breath
& exhale
a streak of cloud
        shaped like a field

       I reach for   try
       to hold
        open palmed—
    like one would a June
bubble from a wand

      but I can't
of course it dissipates
    in an instant,

under the dead branch
of what I think
may be a honey locust.

      Yours.

Citgo Picture

Who, if I cried out.
—Rainer Maria Rilke

At the center
        of it all is the heart.

A stranger
trudging at a truck stop
early morning sleet & light

& the shadow
of the same figure floating
behind him in a floe puddle
like a dead-man
size & color
of his own dark
boot ghosted on the ice.

Looks like
        a guy I might know
but who can be sure
with a face half-masked?

    How winter glooms
& glooms
                        but then I think I hear him
humming (!)
something, climbing
into a snow-wet truck.

    Funny how you can be so
in your own head

writing poems
about pall or daybreak

or wraiths or grief

when a song in a fuel island
under a convenience store
torn awning pinned with glitter
blinking Christmas

                              finds it way like air.

Numbers Going Up Again

                December skyline
        ice-grey
              emptiness.

We are still
protectors in masks.

The scaffolds, city   frozen gunmetal blur.

I pull my scarf closer & coil
my arms around my wire & glass body.

You stand at a distance.

              I don't say anything real
about us because it's too windy & raw
to sit outdoors on the bench with the view
of the Brooklyn Bridge glooming.

The noon sun, too, buries under a cloud cover.

You remember how much
rain fell first time we walked across.

I squint to search the brown wells
that are your eyes.

Your brow a single horizontal line
sure & straight as a tree fallen across a forest bed.

I used to be able to see
the long creek winding in your smile.

        I wish you would come closer.

January wild—

sky shining dark
& violet.

High arborvitaes
wait for snow.

      Tomorrow we will learn of more death.

My boots *crush*
iced-over grass.

A wake of winter
tree jay startle—

star-white—fly.
I find

a tiny periwinkle
holding at the edge

of the lot
& bend to pick

it crushes
on my mitten.

Still, beautiful
crumbled in gravel.

Grandmom's Round Moon Cookies

Mun kichel: poppy seed cookie.

> Everything round.
> The rabbi says we are everything
> turning.

Peasant sweet the hands of my Grandmom

body swaddled
in moon-colored linen
they lay her out in a pine box.

Mystery is boxed in the heart.

Poems of the heart *prepare for death—yet they are not the finish, but the*
> *outset*
>> onset set
>> onset set

> the circular dance
of shape in the sky.

A moon in late afternoon.

In a long motorcade down Woodward
we loop around the zoo.

Glinting jet limousine.

The shape of things.

                    Her patient eyes.

        I once wrote a poem
about a scythe
I keep coming back to
finish.

  Harvest. Wolf Moon.

Sugar—Hunger—Pink Sprouting Grass—Flower & Milk Moon.

Cold Moon.

       These are some of the full moons.

Wolf Peach

June comes too soon
   & blinding.

My tall son
builds a metal obelisk trellis that stands
many feet by the stucco wall.

A baby clematis   opens its way up.

Squinting & blinking
   I've somehow planted

nightshades—eggplant,
sunberries, many-colored
potatoes all along
the walk.

Backyard grape
tomatoes that crave like crazy
the sun,
stems green
furring like a caterpillar.

In my shift of crushed
emerald velvet I am still
          dressed for something dark.

I am always dressed for something dark

as shiny night when the Pink
Blood Moon
looks like a dangerous fruit.

Still Life With Flowering

Here I am

    sun-blind in the back lot
    with mustard flower, sweet
            basil, zinnia

standing like mystery in the wet peat.

A carpenter ant
clamors to a crumb across a field of sun
              on the long rectangle concrete table.

      I trowel
coffee ground compost & gypsum mix

    while the boys in the shorts I washed & dried
            fly their ideas around
                    like box kites

until the wind dies.

Ode to Val, Highest Flower of All

The clematis
on the metal trellis
twigs, snaps, clings,
tendrils.

All summer
I water the vine.

It purples up to the sky.

The morning
              you text me your husband has passed
I stand with the garden hose

   rushing until I make a lake of mud
in my yard.

Then I flood
the entire borough.

People have to climb on their roofs.

But you are so tall
              you see me

dog paddling neck-high in dirt water
& dark velvet violet petals
       from blocks away.

And you swim over.

And you turn the faucet off
with your long,
long arms & save us all.

What Grows

The clematis like mad.

Every petal a different velvet dark
crazy-violet rouge

      hue of July thunder over a field.

Sun-yellow stamens lit like wicks.

Echoes of everything grow.

Words for *love & grief*,
rot, the heat
grows.

    And so what if one plant decomposes
into the next—

        the sky itself grows as I write

     *life is
     but a death-
     bed poem.*

    Mystery stretches when I turn the hose on the vine
& the flower-
      drops like insanely amethyst

prophetesses in the soil.

Still Life With Glitter

August
sits with us at the patio table,
sticking to my legs like my dark glitter
skirt.

Not sure I ever noticed
how pointy the tips of the arborvitaes
are, jagging madness in front of the fence
that separates us
from our neighbors, or
knew how sharp
or immobile words could be
between two people who

                  still love each other.

    I tell my husband I think
the tall trees are giant crayons in a box, but
just the greens—

        cyans, forests,
        thick emeralds.

All different heights.

I remember how
it felt to open a brand-new carton

        how the sharpener
was a promise.

We don't talk about
anything important in the yard

but in late summer the sky
   always blurs
like this

& my metaphors seem
more disjointed
      strangers even to themselves.

A muddle of weeds
tries so hard to be weeds

in the splits between the bluestone.

I tell him
I like the dandelions
& don't want them pulled—

a reminder of something wild
                  & fugitive.

And to please
leave the moss
   velveting green like crazy all over the patio.

Summer Remains
A Poem I Can't Write

Low tide I wander
Paine-Hollow Cove over
    & again
        to see the dolphin

carcass nestling
weeks now in the hummock grass
has eyes eaten
out by shore birds.

Its ribcage exposed
bones white like milkweed.

    How the humidity keeps us
in its grief.

Gnats eddy.
      How my hair coils.

Shoal as a verb means *to make shallow*
    but an inlet
at any tide is a poem
of fullness   unwritten
sun-bleached beach plums
           cattail spikes

& the toxic salve dream of a butterfly weed.

Diamondback terrapin
box turtles make a home
here too—for a time—I

read so in The Gazette
& how they stretch their heads
up from under the seawater
mudflat when it rains   to drink.

I am only a stretching August
shape—there is no word for this
                    although pages are places
we make shadows.

All of us
    only visitors.

        My body under the sun

makes a tall mute slant / passes
across small mounds
of mollusks & rotting
red algae-tangles
    in the sandbar.

Gone to the Larkspurs

Today the sky a picture
    of flowers   blue
bluebells over Brooklyn.

October sun still
flares. Air unfolds,
cools. Street-trees

inside short box fences lonely
gifts lined up, unwrapping
themselves, leaves tinseling.

I shed my flower blue
sweater. Off. On.
Blink & blink.

A black-hatted man hunched
into a curl on a brownstone stoop
has an elm body, neck

like fissured branch with grey
peyos vining
down sides of his face,   ah

my long-dead Grandpop
Abe.   Wild white-red hair.
  Hoeing & watering bent

over potatoes & peppers in his dark fedora
out back of the store, rowhouse color of barley.
Grandpop left the city only

                    this once—
        when we drove in the grocery truck three days without stopping, to see
what stars look like   out west & how wind

    might howl over dry valley wildflowers.
    All of Sixth Avenue is a canyon today.
    A schoolgirl playing Jacks solitaire

    on the sidewalk, small red ball
    hopping haphazardly off
    cracks, clefts, brush.

    The claystone church & second-hand store.
    Wig shop next to wine bar.
    I go in & out

        of grieving so often here—
    freshly born, unnamable
                    exotic smells from a food cart

                incense-around like mountain smoke,
        spicy fruitwood burning its sweet
    ancient sharp.

        Paprika,
            lecso
    so hot we used to cry.

Red Hook

I try to keep clear and still
as water does with the moon.
　　　—Rumi

April clouds are circles like spirits.

The chalk moon in afternoon.

Rectangle containers on a Brooklyn pier.

Rectangle. Rectangle.

Dangling triangle
gantry crane.

I don't feel anything I just
see shapes.

　　Out in the basin the jack-up barge
trapezoid top on long parallel steel legs.

But I can't name a shape for the blue-green water.

　　　　I try to keep clear
　　　　　　and still—

I don't know what I don't know about
love.

　　　　A cormorant on the dock in a parallelepiped
　　　　　　　　of sun,

I try to write
it into a paper-shaped poem.

It goes like the river
as water does with the moon.

Citronella Whispers Dark Lines Into the Night

I slip into my dark glitter
    slip,

        step over the heat, carefully as if
a body moving could somehow cause a thunderstorm to happen

before they say it might
(as if weathermen are ever right).

Summer keeps the city
trapped | waiting for something

spectacularly grieving
& hard to define.

Hangs around the fire escape & yellow
        café lights stringing over Avenue A.

A patio bird taps on cement.

Someone laughs into a napkin.

Order me a whiskey.

        I want to say—*nothing*
    ever dies.

When will it ever begin
        to rain?

The heart always feels so humid
in the eyes.

I'm just over here waiting with my black satin satchel.

Nails the color of tonight
after everything has been turned off.

TWO

Field Guide

If you plant
         yourself in the pitch-
    beautiful graveyard soil behind the back lot
asphalt at the old church
in the new moon,

where legs grow high as a tree.

Mind bed of wild clover.

Will the tall branch to the sun.

Stars are the eyes.

Love is sky.

Rejoice like a weed
                    every hour

the bells will ring.

Taraxacum

Silent girl.

Silent sun.

Silent as a dandelion.

      Faint *growl* of an eight-wheeler   distant silent byway.

   Hush—Ash—Paper Birch—

   Milk-witch.

Her legs silent
skinny stems covered in peat
& florets she drew

         quiet quiet
    on her thigh.

   Brutal mute faint sun.

    Mute-red
rosette of caked blood skinned
knee,
   sweet mute honey mouth.

Silent shock emerald grass.

Silent scream.

     Silent summer
        sacred silent field of wild
    silent witch's gowan

                  & fairy clocks

between the sea of rocks
piled under the deadwood

   silent.

Mary's Gold Field Haiku

Yellow rust red wild
silent shock between wheat shoot,
tobacco, graveyard.

Flashback With Paper Birch & Rock Garden

—after Cynthia Cruz

Then the ambulances arrive screaming.
I'm disguised as a marigold—
And stood under the lush of a white-barked tree.
The day with its kingdom of bees
& scary flowerbed ring-necked snake.
An empty box of Good & Plenty
trampled in peat & sugar ants.
They suctioned my mother's stomach
& wheeled her away.
How I twisted
to the sun, how I stood.
How I glitter my exquisite orange
sorrow in the moss.

Pendant

My childhood friend
Marguerite gave me an amulet
she crafted from a lake oyster
shell found by Erie shore.

I sat in a square of black chestnut
rockery in front of my house with spiky shrubs
pruned into shadows
of shapes, hours
at a time I swung it in the air.

Worn around my neck
the shell was an ancient pond

   the changing color
of a winter bird.

Inside the house
a dark velvet
sorrow & never ending
pacing. Ma
behind her wood door.

Every time
I twisted the braided cord about my wrist
       I could be something
different.

   An ant.
   A waterspout.

Hush of green
moss in a forest
field of trees with pendant drops.

The day I packed
the amulet in my dirt blue roadster & drove

off for good,
Marguerite's eyes were everything.

Her hair a field of butterfly-weed-rushes
in pearl
clasp.

Color of a Roadhouse Porch

Brown closing over the roadhouse, the wild
of the fog-collapse on the lake

Tamarack trees dust rust across the Huron

A blackbird *caws*
like a mystic & the low grey of rain
on an oil drum from the Chevrolet plant
shuttered just downriver

Yellow Corn Moon this far north
deepens as a star to orange

Painted white splintered screen door, iron-
green sign for the state correctional
off the interstate   in the distance

Color of the stranger's story—his
burnt umber field—her midnight blue
        heart—

Yellow moon, yellow moon

on me slanting
in the raked-slat back
of a mountain chair

Red-eyed cicadas by the billions
                buzzing wild.

Prayer Down Depot Road

I can't sleep, America.

The coal cars vibrate, bulky
behind the roadhouse where I stay,
drum by the room at midnight.
At one. Rattle past this insomnia.
A yellow moon stares in the windows.
Spotlight on dreams twisted in a cotton bedcover.
The yellow moon over the railroad shed
shines down the lanky clotheslines,
across cornfields that look like glory
look like patchwork brown flags.
I can't sleep, America.
I can't sleep as if anything matters.
Sing me a song, yellow moon.
An enamel fan, painted-chipped,
whirs the smell of diesel mixed with the sea—
an America poem   poem
                        poem
blowing in & out of my face.

After a Massacre

I believe there are bees still
somewhere in the black tar
cover, over miles of desert
saguaros & mesquite.

Sprays of anemone sprigs twine
into the garland of a bride. She
                shines in some rusted motel
garden gazebo off the Vegas strip.

Just like me to write about leaves
in the middle of a Hellfire.

How I sift through bones for pieces of sky.

This is how I take it
                                even when I can't.

                        I have this woodpecker.
                        It drills & drills
                                rat-a-tat-crack
        on a sugar-water-filled plastic hummingbird feeder
                                in my dark back lot.

                        I have these clouds
                        lined up & piled, one
                        atop another

                        dispelling like morning.
                        They are shaped as bodies.
                        They are shaped as water.

Up-North Rodeway Inn

Farthest stop

up Great Lakes Blue Line

Ice scarring the signal at the shuttered Petoskey station

An electric wire on a fir

Forty-four inches of snow cover Iron Mountain
Speedway down county

Freight cars for miles—
Tonawanda Coke, Howe & Howe—

frozen wait.

A stranger says   *you can hear the cold here*

Hours trancing in the window with winter

sun slanting through the blind
& crewel bird embroidered
dirty curtain   the rays

cut my body
into dark & yellow stripes

Days I listen, try
to hear the mountain.

Poem on a Highway

*

Driving January
snow sloping against the windshield,

glitter field of fences—power
lines—factories—wells.

The kind of dead
beautiful that blankets the bare heart
miles no stopping

*

        Blinding.   I blind.

Reader, I host a séance
under the tallest fir
I find
I don't know
what I yearn to bring back

but *I can't*
not try—

*

Small farmhouse
shows into the distance

        like love lit up under the North Wolf Moon

pitched roof thick with ice & dirt
chimney pumping out smoke
ghost shapes   *ghost shapes*
as far as I can say—

Looking

Tell me the story of the day I was born, I ask a fine pine outside the kitchen door.
Tell me again why I was named Bonnie, I ask a tire swing swinging.

These lost people I search & search for—when I can't find them
around the kitchen counter. When I go looking for my father in a
red velvet casino somewhere down a red velvet street. When I wait
on the bench near the poker pit or in some other ashtray choking.
When I call through the smoke *Daddy, is that you,* when I run out of
ways to run down the freeway screaming, when aortas hook up with
slot machines, red velvet sky pumps down downtown when cashiers
behind ropes *clink clink.* When I yell across *IS THAT YOU* does he
hear me? These lost things do they see me? When my mother can't see
the moon or sea. The empty bottle when I find the phone when they
save her life when she's nearly done when I punch 9-1-1 when I am 9,
or 11. When she stows her sunglasses in the freezer last week. When
she looks for my face in the sink yesterday. When today she turns 85.
When she can't remember a thing. When tomorrow I drop my heart
down the soapy dark dishwater lake to see if it still floats.

Bus Stop Gratiot & Woodward

Out here

no one knows what happens

to the parts of myself I find

stretched across a bench in the heat

on graffiti   over slat

behind some nails.

In this city

no one sees me

pull my heart over my head

& hang it on the side of a warehouse.

I take my legs off too.

Lay them out on cement

next to a book I'm writing,

an ice I'm drinking,

next to a man waiting

for the #34

in a green shirt, printed

shamrocks & vines,

this man in the heat asks me

       are they your pieces or mine

& if I know the way &

       how long?

But it's so hot

I can't hear myself

answer & it's almost as if

       I hallucinate—

this street, this sun,

a sky burning wild.

Valentine's Day

Today I will write about love.

All life I chalk yellow suns onto yellow lines
running down Woodward Ave,
go writing bright green rivers and 1000 hills
into the dark damp gutter sky.

I think about the petrified.
The lost.
The gunned down.

Scribble us all into one perfect
red blood-painted wooden flower cart poem.

I'll just plant roses now under a wet lamppost.
I heart rain.

   Ah there's a pigeon poking around in the weeds and crosswalk
drenched & some tossed off smashed champagne—
me, I'm just a girl waiting

for the DDOT Bus 53.
My legs are getting soaked.

Tomorrow I'll be more prepared for this.
         I'll stick a thesaurus, a laptop
in my waterproof backpack,
wear my parrot yellow waterproof slicker.

I'll sit in the middle of some wet cement & scrawl
                              world, won't you be mine?

Fourth of July Over 8-Mile Road

Tonight the street
          is insomnia red.

Stoplights blinking
roses on cement.

                    The horizon is a ruby—
                    is a prayer—
                    is a lie—

I sell my heart
on this pavement,

tonight the sidewalk
is cherry halogen sky.

                            Crack.
                  crack

          bleed   shimmer.

I give you
all my glitter.

Apollo 11

1

I tell you
again—*an empty bottle*
of Benzos by her bed.

I watch your left eye
shrink from full to half-moon.

It's as if you can't hear me
say—*the ambulance arrived in time,*
she was put in a room
stripped down & without her hairpins
        she looked like no one

I knew. Her pupils
stone-froze
different planets.

2
It's as if you can't hear.

Jimmy's mom looked like an astronaut's wife too.
        Their house near the zoo.

He watched me
fall from the sky
on him in his shag psychedelic room
I wore a mini dress made from a parachute
        stoned-frozen out of my mind.

He tried to hang on while I cried
I am Neil Armstrong in an avalanche
& tethered my legs around his brain
& wondered what on earth could be so fun.

3
It's as if you can't hear me:

I dove heart first into the sea.

Notes

The phrase "prepare for death—yet they are not the finish, but the outset" ("Grandmom's Round Moon Cookies") is from Walt Whitman's "Song of Myself."

Casein is a colloid found in milk that can be combined with water and other solutions to treat a canvas ("In A Squall I Think Washington Square Park is a Jackson Pollock"). Jackson Pollock often mixed oil, enamel, and casein to create his art.

The Latin, scientific name for the common tomato means "Wolf Peach" ("Wolf Peach"). This poem is dedicated to Lynda W and Lynn Ko who dined on the patio the night the poem was born.

Peyos ("Gone To The Larkspurs") is the Hebrew term for the sidelocks worn by some Orthodox Jewish men and boys. *Lecso* is a Hungarian street stew of onions, peppers, tomatoes, and spices.

"Red Hook" is dedicated to Carolina and Peter and *The Mary A. Whalen*, an historic tanker docked in Red Hook, Brooklyn. The word *parallelepiped* is on loan to me from Patrick Donnelly.

Dandelions were once called "fairy clocks" ("Taraxacum"), and *taraxacum* is the Latin word for dandelion.

"Flashback With Paper Birch & Rock Garden" is patterned after Cynthia Cruz's poem "Twelve in Yellow-Weed At The Edge," with her permission.

Tamarack ("Colors of a Roadhouse Porch) is a conifer native to North America, often found in the lake states.

Gratiot Avenue ("Bus Stop At Gratiot & Woodward") is a trunkline starting in Downtown Detroit and running through the city along one of the city's major avenues.

"Apollo 11" is written after Nick Flynn's poem, "You Ask How."

Acknowledgments

My gratitude to the editors of the following journals for first publishing these poems, some in earlier forms or with earlier titles:

American Poetry Review: "Valentine's Day," "Grandmom's Round Moon Cookies," "Dear Winter"

Chiron Review: "Bus Stop At Gratiot & Woodward," "Fourth Of July Over 8-Mile Road"

Colorado Review: "Gone To The Larkspurs"

Great Lakes Review: "Looking," Colors of a Roadhouse Porch"

I-70 Review: "Wolf Peach"

Indolent Books, Poems In The Afterglow: "Citgo Picture," "January wild—"

The Laurel Review: "Citronella Whispers Dark Lines Into the Night"

Mid-American Review: "After A Massacre'

Midwest Review: "Prayer Down Depot Road"

The Night Heron Barks: "In a Squall I Think Washington Square Park is a Jackson Pollock"

Passages North: "Apollo 11"

Ruminate: "Flashback With Paper Birch & Rock Garden"

SWWIM: "The Numbers Going Up Again," "Summer Remains | A Poem I Can't Write"

2 Horatio: "O," "Up-North Roadway Inn

An added thank you to the following prizes who placed this manuscript a finalist:

Idaho Prize for Poetry (Lost Horse Press)
Off the Grid Prize (Grid Books)
Gerald Cable Book Award (Silverfish Review Press)
Hilary Tham Capital Collection (Word Works)

For your perpetual support and fierce reading of this work, thank you to my 2 Horatio poetry dream team: Jennifer Miller, Michele Karas, Sherry Stuart-Berman, Patricia Barnett, Linda Chayes, Joan Capello, Thea Goodman, Joanna Brown, and Vanessa Smith, and to our wise and fearless leader, beloved Elaine Sexton.

To Maja Lukic, my poetry life raft.

To Michelle Valladares, David Groff, and my City College of New York family, who together were a crucial part of this journey.

To my friend Matthew Lippman for first insisting I could publish poems.

For your unconditional love, my Detroit aunts, uncles, and cousins by the dozens, and to my brother Jeffrey, and Ana and Kim, in Kansas City.

Thank you Dr. Ross Tangedal and the University of Wisconsin-Stevens Point for believing in *Glitter City*, and to the entire Cornerstone Press team, including editors Grace Dahl, Carolyn Czerwinski, Ellie Atkinson, and Brett Hill, for your magic.

To Julian.

Bonnie Jill Emanuel is a writer in New York. She holds an MFA in Creative Writing from the City College of New York, where she received the Jerome Lowell DeJur Award in Creative Writing, and the Irwin and Alice Stark Poetry Prize. Her poetry can be found in *American Poetry Review, Colorado Review, Mid-American Review*, and other publications.

Printed in the USA
CPSIA information can be obtained
at www.ICGtesting.com
LVHW042223030224
770832LV00021B/78